From your friends
at
T Bar M Camps

Thanks so much!

Time *with* God *for* FATHERS

by

Jack Countryman

Published in Nashville, Tennessee, by Thomas Nelson. Thomas Nelson is a registered trademark of Thomas Nelson, Inc.

Cover and interior design by Kristy L. Morell, Smyrna, Tennessee.

Thomas Nelson, Inc., titles may be purchased in bulk for educational, business, fund-raising, or sales promotional use. For information, please e-mail *NelsonMinistryServices@ThomasNelson.com*.

Unless otherwise noted, Scripture quotations are taken from THE NEW KING JAMES VERSION. © 1982 by Thomas Nelson, Inc. Used by permission. All rights reserved.

ISBN-13: 978-14041-8945-4
SE ISBN-13: 978-14041-1414-2
SE ISBN-13: 978-14041-8944-7

Printed in China

10 11 12 13 14 RRD 6 5 4 3 2 1

CONTENTS

THE ESSENCE OF WORSHIP

*For the L*ORD *is the great God,*
And the great King above all gods.
In His hand are the deep places of the earth;
The heights of the hills are His also.
The sea is His, for He made it;
And His hands formed the dry land.
Oh come, let us worship and bow down;
*Let us kneel before the L*ORD *our Maker.*
For He is our God,
And we are the people of His pasture,
And the sheep of His hand.

PSALM 95:3–7

*T*o worship your Lord and Heavenly Father is the most wonderful way you can demonstrate the majesty of God. When you open your heart and experience the presence of God in worship, He will speak to you personally. To grow in Christ, it is essential for you to worship your Creator and God. You are His chosen child and He is your sovereign God, who has the power and wisdom to make everything happen in your life that He desires. The Scripture invites you to come, worship, and bow down. Do so often, because He loves you with an everlasting love.

OBEDIENCE IS ESSENTIAL
FOR FATHERS

For the word of God is living and powerful, and
sharper than any two-edged sword, piercing even to
the division of soul and spirit, and of joints and marrow,
and is a discerner of the thoughts and intents of the heart.

HEBREWS 4:12

Obedience is a response that every father desires from his children. When children are obedient to his direction and guidance, there is peace in his home. The same is true with your Heavenly Father. When you obey His commands and abide in His Word, you are blessed and your relationship with God is warm and pursuable. Let God's Word be your daily guide and allow His Spirit to speak to your heart. You, as a father, have been given a great responsibility as priest and leader of your family and home. Be an example of godly obedience to your loved ones.

A FATHER'S PRAYER

Be anxious for nothing, but in everything by prayer and supplication, with thanksgiving, let your requests be made known to God; and the peace of God, which surpasses all understanding, will guard your hearts and minds through Christ Jesus.

PHILIPPIANS 4:6–7

Father, You are more precious to me than life. Thank You for the gift of salvation, which You so generously have given. Forgive me when I have failed to be the father You wish for me to be. Pour out Your Spirit upon me that I might boldly come to the throne of grace and find mercy and power in Your presence. You have blessed me with children and a family; guide me in my words and actions toward them. Shower me with the peace that passes all understanding. Guard my heart and mind so that each day I will be the father You wish for me to be. In Jesus' name, amen.

LISTEN TO THE HOLY SPIRIT

*"If you ask anything in My name, I will do it.
If you love Me, keep My commandments. And I
will pray the Father, and He will give you another Helper,
that He may abide with you forever—the Spirit of truth,
whom the world cannot receive, because it neither sees Him nor
knows Him; but you know Him, for He dwells with you and will
be in you. I will not leave you orphans; I will come to you."*

JOHN 14:14–18

You have been given a Helper. Someone who will be with you in every circumstance of life. This is a promise that God has given to everyone who believes and accepts Jesus as their personal Savior. Learning to listen does not come easily. But when you seek the Lord with all of your heart, His Spirit will be with you to comfort, strengthen, and give you the guidance you want and need in every situation. "If you love Me, keep My commandments" is an essential part of your relationship with God and is necessary for the Holy Spirit to be your comforter and guide. Meditate each day on God's Word, and His Spirit will abide with you forever.

A FATHER'S ETERNAL HOPE

*Blessed be the God and Father of our Lord Jesus
Christ, who according to His abundant mercy has
begotten us again to a living hope through the resurrection
of Jesus Christ from the dead, to an inheritance incorruptible and
undefiled and that does not fade away, reserved in
heaven for you, who are kept by the power of God through
faith for salvation ready to be revealed in the last time.*

1 PETER 1:3–5

Fathers will face certain challenges and times when the
circumstances of life may test your faith. But God has
promised through His abundant mercy that you have a
living and eternal hope in Jesus Christ, and there is no
one or nothing—no challenge or circumstance—that
can take that away. The resurrection of Jesus guarantees
that God will honor all of His promises to His faithful
children. Even when you may find yourself in seemingly
hopeless situations, know that God loves you and He will
make something beautiful out of your life, no matter how
bruised and broken it may be.

WISDOM FOR EACH DAY

Get wisdom! Get understanding!
Do not forget, nor turn away from the words of my mouth.
Do not forsake her, and she will preserve you;
Love her, and she will keep you.
Wisdom is the principal thing;
Therefore get wisdom.
And in all your getting, get understanding.

PROVERBS 4:5–7

Wisdom and understanding are precious commodities, and God encourages us through His Word to seek them. So many times in life, we try to solve life's problems without God's help. God's guidance is more than sufficient for all the tests and trials we might have to face, but in order to benefit from it, we have to seek it out. God has instructed us to come to Him for wisdom. James 1:5 promises, "If any of you lacks wisdom, let him ask of God, who gives to all liberally and without reproach, and it will be given to him." That promise is for you.

THANK GOD FOR FORGIVENESS

Therefore, if anyone is in Christ, he is a new creation; old things have passed away; behold, all things have become new. Now all things are of God, who has reconciled us to Himself through Jesus Christ, and has given us the ministry of reconciliation.

2 CORINTHIANS 5:17–18

When we think about being forgiven, it is like a great weight has been lifted from our shoulders. The beauty of God's forgiveness is that He has promised that our sin will not be remembered ever again. When we belong to Christ, we are His new creation, and the old things which haunt us have passed away. This wonderful gift that God— through His mercy—has given us allows us the freedom to live each day with joy in our hearts and the knowledge that our sins are forgiven. We can then boldly bear witness to the saving grace of our Heavenly Father; therefore, let your light so shine that each of your children may see the love of God in you.

WHEN TROUBLE WALKS
IN YOUR DOOR

Trust in the LORD with all your heart,
And lean not on your own understanding;
In all your ways acknowledge Him,
And He shall direct your paths.

PROVERBS 3:5–6

*T*rouble comes to everyone in all shapes and sizes. But what you *do* with that trouble is all that really matters. Learning to "trust in the Lord with all your heart" is the first step in dealing with trouble. A wise father learns to include God when trouble knocks on his door. God has promised that when you acknowledge Him in all your ways, He will direct your path. God does not intend for you to go through life alone. When you choose to depend on Him for wisdom, He promises to guide your path for His glory and your benefit. You are blessed—even when trouble walks in your door.

WITH GOD THERE IS
NO ROOM FOR FEAR

The Lord is my light and my salvation;
Whom shall I fear?
The Lord is the strength of my life;
Of whom shall I be afraid?

Though an army may encamp against me,
My heart shall not fear;
Though war may rise against me,
In this I will be confident.

PSALM 27:1, 3

*Y*ou do not need to be afraid of anything when the Lord gives you His light. You do not need to fear the power of those who might come against you when you walk in the power of God's Spirit. First John 4:18 says, "perfect love casts out fear." Let each day begin by thanking God for His saving grace and by looking forward to what God's Spirit has planned for you. You will be amazed how that approach to life will affect your entire family, and you will be awed by the blessings you will receive.

COURAGE TO BE A FATHER
OF INTEGRITY

Dishonest scales are an abomination to the LORD,
But a just weight is His delight.
When pride comes, then comes shame;
But with the humble is wisdom.
The integrity of the upright will guide them,
But the perversity of the unfaithful will destroy them.

PROVERBS 11:1–3

*H*onesty and integrity in every area of a father's life is a
blueprint for the man God wishes you to be. This is true
in your personal life, as well as your business practices. The
example you demonstrate for your children will speak vol-
umes and will greatly impact their character development
as they grow into adults. The Lord calls you to do what is
good and right, not only because godly living reflects His
holy character, but also because it benefits and blesses
you. Living honestly for God each day will bring life's
greatest reward.

AS HEAD OF THE HOUSE, THE BUCK STOPS HERE

"Also I say to you, whoever confesses Me before men, him the Son of Man also will confess before the angels of God. But he who denies Me before men will be denied before the angels of God."

LUKE 12:8–9

As a father, you are responsible for the spiritual development of each person in your family. The person that each child becomes will be a reflection of the time and attention you have given that child. Ask God to give you the wisdom, understanding, and patience to guide and direct the physical, emotional, and spiritual development of those He has so graciously given you to nurture and raise. The stamp that you imprint on the character of your loved ones will stay with them for life. May you reflect the godly character you wish each of your children to have.

DO YOU LOVE YOUR NEIGHBOR?

"You shall not bear false witness against your neighbor.
You shall not covet your neighbor's house; you shall
not covet your neighbor's wife, nor his male servant,
nor his female servant, nor his ox, nor his donkey,
nor anything that is your neighbor's."

EXODUS 20:16–17

The love of God and the love of those created in His image form the backbone of everything God says in His Word. When the attitude of love for your neighbor becomes part of your everyday life, caring about others becomes a natural outpouring of God's desire for those who are part of His family. When you as a Christian demonstrate the love of God to your neighbors, you become the person God wishes you to be. God cares for you, so let His love flow from you to your neighbors.

TEACH YOUR CHILDREN EVERY DAY

*Jesus said to him, "'You shall love the LORD your God
with all your heart, with all your soul, and with all
your mind.' This is the first and great commandment.
And the second is like it: 'You shall love your
neighbor as yourself.' On these two commandments
hang all the Law and the Prophets."*

MATTHEW 22:37–40

When learning about God becomes a part of the daily
habits of a family, the Christian life and character will
naturally grow and create the love for God's Word that is
so essential in the Christian development of your children.
God loves for you to use nature and His beauty around
you as a ready source of spiritual object lessons. While
observing nature is no substitute for spending time in His
Word, it can open your eyes to spiritual truth in a way
nothing else does. Take time each day to point out the
power of God's presence all around you.

EVERYTHING BEGINS WITH TRUST

And he said:
"The LORD is my rock and my fortress and my deliverer;
The God of my strength, in whom I will trust;
My shield and the horn of my salvation,
My stronghold and my refuge;
My Savior, You save me from violence.

2 SAMUEL 22:2–3

The word *trust* is mentioned in the Bible over fifty times. God asks you to "Trust in the Lord with all your heart" (Proverbs 3:5). When you learn to accept this command, you can face any circumstance with confidence and hope because it is not your strength, wisdom, energy, or power that brings victory in life. Triumph comes because of God's ability, and when you place your trust in Him, you tap into an irresistible force that no one or nothing can successfully oppose.

GRATITUDE BEGINS WITH ATTITUDE

Finally, brethren, whatever things are true,
whatever things are noble, whatever things are just,
whatever things are pure, whatever things are lovely,
whatever things are of good report, if there is any virtue and if
there is anything praiseworthy—meditate on these things.

PHILIPPIANS 4:8

*H*ave you ever had someone say, "You need to change your attitude"? How we approach the challenges of life determines the kind of person we become. If we ponder negative things, our frame of mind will soon turn sour, pessimistic, and negative. If we fill our minds with the things of God, however, the opposite will occur, and we will begin to see the world as God sees it. God wants us to be transformed into people who love to please Him through willing obedience. That transformation begins in the mind and transcends into an attitude of gratitude.

KINDNESS IS CONTAGIOUS

"Or what man is there among you who, if his son asks for bread, will give him a stone? Or if he asks for a fish, will he give him a serpent? If you then, being evil, know how to give good gifts to your children, how much more will your Father who is in heaven give good things to those who ask Him!"

MATTHEW 7:9–11

A father who has a kind and tender heart will be a magnet to those whom he loves, especially to those in his immediate family. Everyone craves love and encouragement. When you demonstrate your love through kindness and a caring heart, you build confidence, security, and a foundation of trust for your family that will not be broken. As God demonstrates His love, grace, and mercy to you each day, so let your words and actions daily reflect that same love, grace, and mercy to each of your children.

THE COMFORT ONLY GOD CAN GIVE

Blessed be the God and Father of our Lord Jesus Christ, the Father of mercies and God of all comfort, who comforts us in all our tribulation, that we may be able to comfort those who are in any trouble, with the comfort with which we ourselves are comforted by God. For as the sufferings of Christ abound in us, so our consolation also abounds through Christ.

2 CORINTHIANS 1:3–5

The "God of all comfort." These are truly encouraging words. When trials and unexpected situations come into your life, you may ask "Why?" But never doubt that God will come to your aid, because that is His promise for those who follow Christ. He is the Father of all mercy and the One "who comforts us in all our tribulation." He will see you through whatever trials you may be facing. He will then use those experiences to train you, in turn, to be a comfort to those around you.

THE STRENGTH ONLY GOD CAN GIVE

For I am persuaded that neither death nor life, nor angels nor
principalities nor powers, nor things present nor things to come,
nor height nor depth, nor any other created thing, shall be able to
separate us from the love of God which is in Christ Jesus our Lord.

ROMANS 8:38–39

A father's life is filled with joy, happiness, peace, challenge, trials, sorrow, worry, fear, and doubt. These are the common adjectives of every father's life. But once you accept God's love through faith in Jesus Christ, nothing can break the bonds of that love He creates. John 10:29 says, "no one is able to snatch them out of My Father's hand." Begin each day by praising God for His love, and look forward to sharing His love with each precious soul God has given you to nurture and raise.

PEACE AND ANGER ARE
LIKE OIL AND WATER

*Now I plead with you, brethren, by the name of our
Lord Jesus Christ, that you all speak the same thing, and
that there be no divisions among you, but that you be perfectly
joined together in the same mind and in the same judgment.*

1 CORINTHIANS 1:10

When anger and discord become a continual visitor to
your home, there will not be a place for peace within the
family. Peace will walk out the back door. The family is
called to be of one mind and one spirit. A father's role is
to make sure this happens. You are the spiritual leader and
the one who is called to keep everything within the family
in balance. Accept the role God has given you, and create
the bond of love that cannot be broken. You will be blessed
for your efforts.

DISCIPLINE IS A
FATHER'S RESPONSIBILITY

Foolishness is bound up in the heart of a child;
The rod of correction will drive it far from him.

PROVERBS 22:15

Discipline and correction oftentimes do not come easily
to a loving father. It is not a pleasant experience for anyone
in the family. Yet, the Bible speaks clearly about discipline
in Proverbs 13:24, saying that "He who spares his rod hates
his son, But he who loves him disciplines him promptly."
We all need correction at many points, and your children
need to learn what is and is not acceptable in life. If not,
they will go down the wrong path and end up at the wrong
destination. A firm, loving hand today will be the building
block for tomorrow.

GOD GIVES A FATHER STRENGTH
WHEN FAMILIES GROW APART

Therefore my spirit is overwhelmed within me;
My heart within me is distressed.

Answer me speedily, O LORD;
My spirit fails!
Do not hide Your face from me,
Lest I be like those who go down into the pit.
Cause me to hear Your lovingkindness in the morning,
For in You do I trust;
Cause me to know the way in which I should walk,
For I lift up my soul to You.

PSALM 143:4, 7–8

*S*ometimes in life—and for various reasons—families fall apart. At that point, every emotion imaginable enters into your life, leaving you hurt, broken, confused, and wondering how in the world this could possibly happen to you. God stands ready to give you His guidance—and you need to recognize that we all need it every day. He will instruct you if you ask for it. You must ask in faith and then be willing to listen carefully to His voice. He will guide you when you are truly ready to follow. Be willing to look beyond your ego and emotion, and depend on the One who loves you with an everlasting love. He is the perfect Healer for your broken heart.

21

A FATHER'S CHALLENGE: GROW IN YOUR CHRISTIAN WALK

Teach me, O LORD, the way of Your statutes,
And I shall keep it to the end.
Give me understanding, and I shall keep Your law;
Indeed, I shall observe it with my whole heart.
Make me walk in the path of Your commandments,
For I delight in it.

PSALM 119:33–35

*I*f you want to please God and honor Him with your life, you must get to know His Word. The Bible warns us of the challenges we may face, steers us toward the heart of God, and gives us the wisdom to flourish in every situation we may face. Many Christian fathers have never experienced the power and encouragement available to them through studying God's Word and memorizing Scripture. But when you lock portions of God's Word in your mind, they remain available always to help you in tough times. Begin today, and let God's Word strengthen your Christian walk.

A FATHER'S CHARACTER BEGINS
WITH HONESTY

Lying lips are an abomination to the LORD,
But those who deal truthfully are His delight.

PROVERBS 12:22

The Bible clearly states that God always keeps His promises. In other words, He always speaks the truth. When a father can be trusted to speak the truth in every circumstance, he builds a bond of trust that pleases God and everyone in his family. Proverbs 13:3 says, "He who guards his mouth preserves his life, But he who opens wide his lips shall have destruction." Guard your words with those you love, for they are watching your character as you try to build up theirs.

FORGIVENESS IS A TRAIT GOD LOVES

Repay no one evil for evil. Have regard for good
things in the sight of all men. If it is possible, as much
as depends on you, live peaceably with all men.

ROMANS 12:17–18

Forgiveness is an essential element in living the Christian life. When you choose to forgive someone who has hurt you or disappointed you, the window of God's forgiveness will open to comfort and heal your own heart. Everything you do should reflect well on the Savior who bought you with His own blood. Pleasing God with your words and deeds opens heaven's door to bless your life for His glory. If God has forgiven you of your transgressions—"As far as the east is from the west" (Psalm 103:12)—should you not do the same for anyone who has offended you?

GOD CHALLENGES FATHERS TO SHOW THEIR FAITH

And let us not grow weary while doing good,
for in due season we shall reap if we do not lose
heart. Therefore, as we have opportunity, let us do good
to all, especially to those who are of the household of faith.

GALATIANS 6:9–10

A father is the spiritual leader and mentor of his family. The faith he demonstrates in his heavenly Father will set the stage for the spiritual climate of the home. The goal for Christian living for everyone in the home is not to sin less or to reform our manners or to do better than we used to. The goal is total transformation, to be transformed into the likeness of Jesus. God wants us to increasingly resemble His Son. When your faith becomes the guiding light of your life, you will have God's blessing.

WHO IS THE OWNER OF
YOUR TREASURE?

*"So that you do not appear to men to be fasting, but to
your Father who is in the secret place; and your
Father who sees in secret will reward you openly.
Do not lay up for yourselves treasures on earth, where moth and
rust destroy and where thieves break in and steal; but lay up for
yourselves treasures in heaven, where neither moth nor rust de-
stroys and where thieves do not break in and steal. For where your
treasure is, there your heart will be also."*

MATTHEW 6:18–21

*T*reasure is a word most people relate to money, power,
and possessions, as well as the achievements attained in the
business world. But, let us consider another aspect of *treasure*. What do you think about during the day? What gets
your heart beating fastest and loudest? What do you think
you could not live without? Whatever it is, that is your
treasure—and nothing but God is worth it. Too many
times we try and serve two masters—God and works or
God and the bank account—but Jesus said it's impossible
to serve two masters (see Matthew 6:24). When you store
up your treasure in heaven, your heart will follow.

ACCOUNTABILITY IS AN ABSOLUTE FOR FATHERS

Two are better than one,
Because they have a good reward for their labor.
For if they fall, one will lift up his companion.
But woe to him who is alone when he falls,
For he has no one to help him up.

ECCLESIASTES 4:9–10

The idea of being accountable to someone for our actions in life is often like sandpaper rubbing our egos raw. God never calls on any of His children to "go it alone" in their walk with Him. We need each other not only to receive help and encouragement, but also to remain transparent with our loved ones and those whom God has brought into our lives. When we are honest with God *and* with a trusted Christian friend, the commitment we have for a deeper walk with the Savior becomes a spiritual bond that will not be broken.

LORD, HEAR MY PRAYER

"Ask, and it will be given to you; seek, and you will find; knock, and it will be opened to you. For everyone who asks receives, and he who seeks finds, and to him who knocks it will be opened."

MATTHEW 7:7–8

*L*ord, You have asked me to come to You with an open heart, to seek You and find what is Your will for my life. Help me to be open and sincere with all that I am for Your glory. Through Your grace and goodness, lead me to a deeper, richer relationship with You. Mold me, O Lord, to be the father You wish me to be. Fill me with Your wisdom and understanding so that Your Word will come alive in my life. Place Your hand upon me so that Your Spirit will be my constant guide and so that You may be glorified in all that I say and do. May You forever be praised. Amen.

FATHER, HELP ME TO BE PATIENT

For even Christ did not please Himself; but as it is written, "The reproaches of those who reproached You fell on Me." For whatever things were written before were written for our learning, that we through the patience and comfort of the Scriptures might have hope. Now may the God of patience and comfort grant you to be like-minded toward one another, according to Christ Jesus.

ROMANS 15:3–5

*P*atience has been defined as learning to accept difficult situations without giving God a deadline for their removal. We know we need patience, but we generally shun the process by which we learn it. We want it now! We cannot wait for God's direction, so we move ahead on our own initiative. The Old Testament admonishes us, "Wait on the LORD; Be of good courage, And He shall strengthen your heart; Wait, I say, on the LORD!" (Psalm 27:14). The Bible promises that trials and tribulations will produce patience as you learn to endure, to bear up, to persevere, and to keep holding on with no worldly help in sight. If you do so, God will grant you all the patience you need.

THE HOLY SPIRIT WILL
BE YOUR GUIDE

*"And I will pray the Father, and He will give you
another Helper, that He may abide with you
forever—the Spirit of truth, whom the world cannot
receive, because it neither sees Him nor knows Him; but
you know Him, for He dwells with you and will be in you."*

JOHN 14:16–17

To whom do you turn for daily guidance on how to live, what to do, where to go, whom to see, how to make decisions? The Scriptures say the only guide worth trusting is the Holy Spirit. He is the only One who knows your past completely, from the moment you were conceived to the present, and who knows your future from this day to eternity. Only He knows God's plan and purpose for you, what is fully good and right for you. The Spirit of truth is the inner compass for your life, pointing you toward what Jesus would be, say, or do in any given moment. God desires to make His will known to you; He wants you to know what to do and when to do it. And He gives you this knowledge through the indwelling of the Holy Spirit. Trust the Holy Spirit to be your daily guide.

CONFESSION OF SIN DOES NOT COME EASY—HELP, LORD!

The LORD is far from the wicked,
But He hears the prayer of the righteous.
The light of the eyes rejoices the heart,
And a good report makes the bones healthy.
The ear that hears the rebukes of life
Will abide among the wise.
He who disdains instruction despises his own soul,
But he who heeds rebuke gets understanding.
The fear of the LORD is the instruction of wisdom,
And before honor is humility.

PROVERBS 15:29–33

A father's pride and ego is like a wall that separates him from the will of God, and that wall is not easily broken down. When you believe you are self-sufficient and need not answer to anyone, Satan will have his way in your life. When you become self-absorbed and listen to no one, there is no room for God to come in and change you for His glory. The Bible clearly says in 1 John 1:9, "If we confess our sins, He is faithful and just to forgive us our sins and to cleanse us from all unrighteousness." Let nothing interfere with your confession; let go of your ego and pride. God wants to restore you to His family today. His grace is sufficient and nothing can take that away. Praise God!

THE JOY OF PRAISING THE LORD

I will extol You, my God, O King;
And I will bless Your name forever and ever.
Every day I will bless You,
And I will praise Your name forever and ever.
Great is the Lord, and greatly to be praised;
And His greatness is unsearchable.
One generation shall praise Your works to another,
And shall declare Your mighty acts.

PSALM 145:1–4

When life with its twists and turns takes you down unexpected and difficult roads, it can sometimes feel strange to praise the Lord. Yet, He seeks your praise in all things—whether they appear good to us or not. Remember that God is good and always gives ample reason to praise Him. God's overriding purpose for your life is to glorify Him, and He will use any means to accomplish that. Ask Him to open your heart so that you will see your life's circumstances as He does. Psalm 146:2 says, "While I live I will praise the Lord; I will sing praises to my God while I have my being." Despite how you may feel, praise can flow from you like a fountain—beginning right now.

CHILDREN ARE A JOY
FROM THE LORD

*"You are the salt of the earth; but if the salt loses its flavor,
how shall it be seasoned? It is then good for nothing but
to be thrown out and trampled underfoot by men.
You are the light of the world. A city that is set on a hill
cannot be hidden. Nor do they light a lamp and put it
under a basket, but on a lampstand, and it gives light to all
who are in the house. Let your light so shine before men, that
they may see your good works and glorify your Father in heaven."*

MATTHEW 5:13–16

Jesus wants you to take seriously your role as a father. As "salt," your behavior is to be distinctly different from those who do not know God, and it must not reflect the same kind of behavior that corrupts a godless culture. Do your children see that you are burning with the light of heaven? What "good works" do they see you doing that reflect well on your heavenly Father? How does your faith cause you to behave differently from anyone else? Let your light shine brightly for God, and He will bless you beyond your greatest imaginings.

GOD FILLS FATHERS WITH JOY
WHEN THEY WORSHIP HIM

"But the hour is coming, and now is, when the true worshipers will worship the Father in spirit and truth; for the Father is seeking such to worship Him. God is Spirit, and those who worship Him must worship in spirit and truth."

JOHN 4:23–24

God is looking for men who will eagerly worship Him, according to the truth of the Scripture and the power of the Holy Spirit. In order for you to have an intimate relationship with God, it is essential that you come to Him with an open heart, willing to surrender your life and worship Him in truth and in spirit. Bringing glory to God will refresh your own spirit and draw you closer to the heavenly Father. Make worshiping God a part of your character-building walk with Him. The impact that you will have on those you love will fill your heart with a deep sense of satisfaction and give you a peace that passes all understanding.

SECURITY IS GUARANTEED WHEN
THE LORD IS NUMBER ONE

My son, if you receive my words,
And treasure my commands within you,
So that you incline your ear to wisdom,
And apply your heart to understanding;

Yes, if you cry out for discernment,
And lift up your voice for understanding,
If you seek her as silver,
And search for her as for hidden treasures;
Then you will understand the fear of the LORD,
And find the knowledge of God.

PROVERBS 2:1–5

*S*ecurity and wisdom are like Siamese twins—one cannot accomplish anything without the other. The more we know and understand God's Word, the more secure we can feel in our walk with God. So many times we fail to seek God's wisdom, and we strive to satisfy our passions and desires without regard to the future or the consequences of our decisions. In this life, tests will come in all shapes and sizes. Some will require us to endure. Some we will anticipate, while others will blindside us. All of them ask us to make the right decisions. Regardless of the test, God instructs us to come to Him for the wisdom we so desperately need.

THERE IS NO WORRY OR DOUBT
WHEN YOU WALK WITH GOD

The LORD is righteous in all His ways,
Gracious in all His works.
The LORD is near to all who call upon Him,
To all who call upon Him in truth.
He will fulfill the desire of those who fear Him;
He also will hear their cry and save them.
The LORD preserves all who love Him,
But all the wicked He will destroy.
My mouth shall speak the praise of the LORD,
And all flesh shall bless His holy name
Forever and ever.

PSALM 145:17–21

Worry is a killer in the spiritual life of a Christian. When worry walks in your door, doubt will soon follow. God is the great Provider. Do not look to God merely hoping for what you need, but rather expecting. Put your hope in His great love, and worry will eventually disappear as you take your concerns to God, who has the power and wisdom to take care of them. Trust that He always has your best interest at heart.

PERFECT LOVE CASTS OUT ALL FEAR

*"Be strong and of good courage, do not fear nor be afraid of them; for the L*ORD *your God, He is the One who goes with you. He will not leave you nor forsake you."*

DEUTERONOMY 31:6

The Scripture reminds us in 1 John 4:18 that "There is no fear in love; but perfect love casts out fear." The love of God is not merely a warm sentiment or a pleasant feeling; it is a living, active force that changes who we are. Jesus Himself forever connected the love of God to His love of people. God continually reminds us that He is right there with us in both the easiest of times and the most difficult of times. When you feel afraid or uncertain about the future, let your spirit be lifted as you remind yourself of the loving character of God.

GOD WILL COMFORT YOU WHEN LOVED ONES ARE SICK

Is anyone among you sick? Let him call for the elders of the church, and let them pray over him, anointing him with oil in the name of the Lord. And the prayer of faith will save the sick, and the Lord will raise him up. And if he has committed sins, he will be forgiven.

JAMES 5:14–15

The recognition of God's power to heal your loved ones is a key component to experiencing His tender love. Do you look for comfort? Paul writes in 2 Corinthians 1:3–4, "Blessed be the God and Father of our Lord Jesus Christ, the Father of mercies and God of all comfort, who comforts us in all our tribulation, that we may be able to comfort those who are in any trouble, with the comfort with which we ourselves are comforted by God." There is no such thing as life without sickness and pain. But God has promised to be with you in sickness and in health. As God ministers to you at these times, let Him equip you to be a comfort to those you love when they need you.

DISCIPLINE AND LOVE GO HAND-IN-HAND

*Furthermore, we have had human fathers who corrected
us, and we paid them respect. Shall we not much more
readily be in subjection to the Father of spirits and live?
For they indeed for a few days chastened us as seemed best
to them, but He for our profit, that we may be partakers of His
holiness. Now no chastening seems to be joyful for the present,
but painful; nevertheless, afterward it yields the peaceable
fruit of righteousness to those who have been trained by it.*

HEBREWS 12:9–11

No one likes to be disciplined, particularly adults. It
never feels good and rarely puts a smile on our face or a
spring in our step. But when we choose to cooperate with
God as He corrects us, blessings always come. Our eyes
and hearts are opened to His mercy and grace, and we
are blessed with the opportunity for a closer walk with
Him. When God is working in and through us, His Spirit
enables us to do worthwhile things for the Kingdom.
When we obey God and do His will and please Him, we
can truly do all things through Christ whose Spirit dwells
within us.

GOD'S SPECIAL LOVE
FOR TROUBLED FATHERS

*In this you greatly rejoice, though now for a little while,
if need be, you have been grieved by various trials, that
the genuineness of your faith, being much more precious than
gold that perishes, though it is tested by fire, may be found to
praise, honor, and glory at the revelation of Jesus Christ, whom
having not seen you love. Though now you do not see Him,
yet believing, you rejoice with joy inexpressible and full of glory.*

1 PETER 1:6–8

God knows you face difficult situations. He hears your cries. Even those who maintain the closest fellowship with Him are not immune to feelings of hopelessness when problems seem overwhelming. Sometimes, God allows you to face impossible circumstances in order to test your faith. When there is no other place to turn, you are forced to seek God, and it is there you will find strength and the very answers you need. God knows exactly what you need to solve your problems and to bring you into a more intimate relationship with Him. If you will let Him, He will take your life—no matter how battered and stained—and make something beautiful out of it for His glory.

GOD WILL HELP YOU GUIDE YOUR CHILDREN

"Fear not, for I am with you;
Be not dismayed, for I am your God.
I will strengthen you,
Yes, I will help you,
I will uphold you with My righteous right hand."

ISAIAH 41:10

God has promised that His grace is sufficient for any need that you may have. As a father, the security and strength that your children need comes from your willingness to build a bond of love and confidence that cannot be broken. Each of us has faced fear at some point in life; it is what we do with that fear that matters most. You must claim your position as a child of God, who has been given the Holy Spirit as your guide and protector. Apply God's Word to your life, and it will give you the power to overcome fear.

GOD'S LOVE FOR FATHERS WHEN THEY FORGIVE THEIR CHILDREN

The LORD is merciful and gracious,
Slow to anger, and abounding in mercy.
He will not always strive with us,
Nor will He keep His anger forever.
He has not dealt with us according to our sins,
Nor punished us according to our iniquities.
For as the heavens are high above the earth,
So great is His mercy toward those who fear Him;
As far as the east is from the west,
So far has He removed our transgressions from us.

PSALM 103:8–12

When you forgive your children for something they have done that has been disappointing and hurtful, you are emulating exactly what your heavenly Father does when you fail to live up to His standard for your life. Forgiveness breaks down the walls that separate you from the love of your children, and it opens the door to reconciliation. The unconditional love that your heavenly Father has promised to you is the same kind of love needed by those God has given you to nurture and raise. Let nothing interfere with God's gracious gift of forgiveness, and the reward you receive will bless you richly.

THE BLESSINGS OF TRUST
IN THE LORD

My soul, wait silently for God alone,
For my expectation is from Him.
He only is my rock and my salvation;
He is my defense;
I shall not be moved.
In God is my salvation and my glory;
The rock of my strength,
And my refuge, is in God.

PSALM 62:5–7

No matter where you travel in life, or what challenges you may face as a father, the Rock of God goes before you, inviting you to "Trust in the Lord with all your heart" (Proverbs 3:5). When you hand your troubled emotions to Him, He will always be there. Let nothing separate you from the love of Christ. Depend on His Spirit to give you strength and to guide you every day through whatever life may bring. God's desire for your family is that each one will know the loving grace and mercy that only He can give. Let each day be filled with the power of His presence as you trust in the Lord to give you His wisdom and understanding.

JESUS AND YOU

"I am the vine, you are the branches. He who abides in Me, and I in him, bears much fruit; for without Me you can do nothing. If anyone does not abide in Me, he is cast out as a branch and is withered; and they gather them and throw them into the fire, and they are burned. If you abide in Me, and My words abide in you, you will ask what you desire, and it shall be done for you."

JOHN 15:5–7

The relationship you have with Jesus Christ is the most important relationship you will ever have. When you belong to Christ, you have been called to play a significant role in the kingdom of God. This role can only be fulfilled if you allow Jesus to live His life in and through you. While apart from Him, you can do nothing; in Him, you can do anything He calls you to do. Jesus did not want you to lead an unproductive or unfocused life. He chose you not only for salvation, but also to fulfill a specific purpose for the glory of Him and His kingdom.

YOU CAN COUNT ON EVERY PROMISE GOD HAS MADE

"Behold, this day I am going the way of all the earth. And you know in all your hearts and in all your souls that not one thing has failed of all the good things which the LORD your God spoke concerning you. All have come to pass for you; not one word of them has failed."

JOSHUA 23:14

The Bible contains several thousand promises that were created so that you can be secure in trusting God's Word to have the answers you need in times of difficulty and hardship. When you walk with God, He promises to "never leave you nor forsake you" (Hebrews 13:5). He also promises that when you "delight yourself also in the LORD," then "He shall give you the desires of your heart" (Psalm 37:4). God desires a close relationship with those who call Him Lord and who have given their lives to Him. Each of God's promises is designed to help you grow in your faith, draw closer to Him, and trust that He will guide and direct your life.

NICE GUYS ALWAYS WIN IN THE END

Therefore, as the elect of God, holy and beloved, put on tender mercies, kindness, humility, meekness, longsuffering.

COLOSSIANS 3:12

When a father learns to depend on God for wisdom, insight, and understanding, he *always* wins! One of the key lessons of life is to recognize that, without God, life will be a struggle, and no one wins. But with God all things are possible. Many times we allow our selfish ambitions to influence who we become and how we live. During these times money, material possessions, and personal power become the center of our attention, and our relationship with God is either forgotten or takes a backseat to our own desires for our lives. When this happens, we lose spiritually. God will not settle for last place; He wants to be first in your heart. In order to win spiritually, you must lose yourself completely in the will of the Lord.

LET YOUR GREATEST LOVE BE GOD

*"Therefore know that the L*ORD *your God, He is God, the faithful God who keeps covenant and mercy for a thousand generations with those who love Him and keep His commandments."*

DEUTERONOMY 7:9

*E*verything you do and don't do, face and don't face is touched by God's continuing love. Everything about you is hinged on love, because God—who is love—created you in His image. And because God loves you, He gives you blessings and lets you share them. When you pray and are told to wait, it is because He loves you and knows you need time to grow. When the overwhelming choices before you make it hard to know which way is up, our Lord and Savior shows you your need to depend on His guiding love. Until you come to understand and believe at your deepest, innermost level that God *is* love, you will struggle with trusting Him, obeying Him, and seeking Him wholeheartedly. One of the keys to your spiritual growth is believing in God's love, even when you cannot see it.

FOCUS IS THE NAME OF THE GAME

"'And you shall love the LORD your God with all your heart, with all your soul, with all your mind, and with all your strength.' This is the first commandment. And the second, like it, is this: 'You shall love your neighbor as yourself.' There is no other commandment greater than these."

MARK 12:30–31

When you talk about being a Christian and living the Christian life, everything hinges on the first two commandments. There is first the vertical commandment to love the Lord with all of your heart, soul, mind, and strength. Then the second is a horizontal commandment to love your neighbor as yourself. The essence of these verses is love—love for God and for each other. It is the kind of love that seeks no reward or personal gain, but rather desires to honor God by sharing His grace and generosity with those around you. Great character and good morals are built on this foundation and, when practiced in everyday life, the Lord is lifted up and you are blessed.

LOOKING AT OTHERS
THROUGH JESUS' EYES

Therefore receive one another, just as Christ
also received us, to the glory of God.

ROMANS 15:7

The attitude and influence we choose to have with our brothers and sisters in Christ is often determined by how we receive those whom we see in church every week. When God looks at each of us through the eyes of Jesus, He sees us as perfect because Jesus has paid the price for all of our sins. The Scripture asks us, in turn, to receive one another without fault or judgment. When this takes place, the barriers that stunt our relationship with other Christians are removed and fellowship becomes the joy of our hearts. This attitude is the foundation for building a solid relationship with those whom we call the body of Christ.

A FATHER'S LIFE WITH NO REGRETS

For the Scripture says, "Whoever believes on Him will not be put to shame." For there is no distinction between Jew and Greek, for the same Lord over all is rich to all who call upon Him.

ROMANS 10:11–12

*B*ecoming a father is a gift that only God can give. Through His divine providence, you have been given the privilege of having children. Accept the blessing and look forward to the adventure of raising your children with the love of God in their hearts. When you place your faith in Christ, His Spirit will be ever-present to guide you to be the best father you can be. He wants very much to be included in your daily life as a parent and as a follower of Jesus Christ. God never offers salvation to you and then pulls the rug out from under you. When you put your faith in Christ, everything you need to be a great father is available. You need only to ask and God, through His gracious mercy, will deliver.

A FATHER'S FAITH IS THE KEY TO IT ALL

*But without faith it is impossible to please Him,
for he who comes to God must believe that He is, and
that He is a rewarder of those who diligently seek Him.*

HEBREWS 11:6

The beautiful thing about faith is that it declares our weakness, while at the same time it proclaims the strength and trustworthiness of God and His complete and willing ability to do what we cannot. A lack of faith insults God, even as it puts foolish confidence in our own abilities. Faith is not wishful thinking or believing what we know isn't true, it is the conviction that God will always do what He promises to do, regardless of the circumstances we are facing in life.

THE CHOICE IS YOURS:
GOD OR MONEY

"No one can serve two masters; for either he will hate the one and love the other, or else he will be loyal to the one and despise the other. You cannot serve God and mammon."

MATTHEW 6:24

So many times in life we struggle with our priorities and our choices, our needs and our wants. It is too easy to end up serving more than one master and find there is little satisfaction from either. When you have two masters—such as God and work, or God and bank accounts, or God and family—all of which have contradicting demands, you must make a choice about whom you will serve. When your life comes together and everything you desire places God first, the choices you must make will come easily.

AN ORDINARY MAN SERVING GOD IS AN EXTRAORDINARY FATHER

For we are His workmanship, created in Christ Jesus for good works, which God prepared beforehand that we should walk in them.

EPHESIANS 2:10

The wonderful message about God is that we were all created in His image and He believes that we are all extraordinary. God knows you perfectly and loves you completely, just the way you are. You are His masterpiece—His workmanship of grace and love, His work of art. As you grow, He continues to paint the portrait of your life in such a way that you will glorify Him. Many times, this is a hard concept to grasp, since you see your life as incomplete, an unfinished portrait. But His eternal eyes know exactly where you need His greatest attention. Every frustration, every disappointment, and every joy is a brushstroke, serving a purpose in God's perfect plan. In His eyes, you are a masterpiece.

LIVING FOR GOD FROM
THE INSIDE OUT

Therefore we do not lose heart. Even though our outward man is perishing, yet the inward man is being renewed day by day.

2 CORINTHIANS 4:16

Living for God from the inside out begins with a change of heart and your decision to be a different person. The way you walk, talk, and interact with your family and friends will change as you are called to reflect Jesus Christ in every area of your life. When you become a Christian, you assume a personal responsibility to live for Christ. Although your sins have been forgiven through Christ's sacrifice, you are still responsible for your behavior. What you do on earth matters. You are free in Christ, but you are also bondservants of Christ. Pleasing God is to be your first priority. And as a Christian father, who you are in Christ will be reflected in your children as they observe the way you live—from the inside out.

THE LONG WALK HOME

Though now you do not see Him, yet believing, you
rejoice with joy inexpressible and full of glory, receiving
the end of your faith—the salvation of your souls.

1 PETER 1:8–9

The Christian life is intended to be both a joyful experience and serious business. It takes a conscious, deliberate, Spirit-filled action to ponder God's grace and Jesus' return in such a way that it positively shapes how we live. How could we not have joy in our hearts when we know that God loves us, is with us, promises to help us, and wants to bless us forever? Let your own long walk home be in step with the One who loves you with an everlasting love.

LOOKING OUT FOR NUMBER TWO

*Let nothing be done through selfish ambition or
conceit, but in lowliness of mind let each esteem others
better than himself. Let each of you look out not only for
his own interests, but also for the interests of others.*

PHILIPPIANS 2:3–4

*I*n today's culture, looking out for "Number Two" is not a popular lifestyle. Personal desires and self-ambition are the driving force in the way most of us think and live. This lifestyle is the direct opposite of what God desires for those who are in Christ. With every step you take, every decision you make, every conversation you have, every thought you entertain, the Lord desires to live within you. He desires to live out His life through your experience of it; a blend of His perfection and your unique talents, traits, and personality. Living for Jesus Christ is all about caring for others more than you care about yourself. Start today!

GOD HAS PROMISED YOU WILL NEVER BE ALONE

Now may our Lord Jesus Christ Himself, and our God and Father, who has loved us and given us everlasting consolation and good hope by grace, comfort your hearts and establish you in every good word and work.

2 THESSALONIANS 2:16–17

The Bible repeatedly tells us in both the Old and New Testaments that God will never leave us nor forsake us. We can take this to heart because God's promises are true. His ways are everlasting, as He shares with us in Malachi 3:6a, "For I am the LORD, I do not change." The Lord will remain the same forever. Include Him in every aspect of your life, both when times are good and when they are stressful. You can trust in Him to be your Comforter, your strength in times of trouble, and the One you can turn to when no one else will listen.

HONOR BEGINS WITH GOD

Honor the LORD with your possessions,
And with the firstfruits of all your increase;
So your barns will be filled with plenty,
And your vats will overflow with new wine.

PROVERBS 3:9–10

*I*t is difficult for some people to accept that every posses-
sion belongs to God. Just as He graciously gives us good
things every day, we should look for ways to bless others,
demonstrating to the world the boundless love of God.
When we choose to honor God with all that we have and
provide a way to bless those who are struggling in life, we
become true servants of our living God. God is constantly
watching over us, noting our decisions, pondering our
plans, and observing our behavior. He knows exactly what
we need, and so invites us to ask Him for His counsel. He
is waiting to bless you with His love and grace.

IN GOD'S EYES, LESS IS MORE

And He said to them, "Take heed and beware of covetousness, for one's life does not consist in the abundance of the things he possesses."

LUKE 12:15

So many times in life we get sidetracked with our grownup toys and material possessions. True satisfaction in life flows out of fulfilling the purpose for which we were created: to enjoy an intimate relationship with God. Acquiring material excess as a substitute for a real relationship with God only makes the heart feel hollow and empty. The example you portray for your children about the importance of a relationship with God, compared to gaining material wealth, will set the stage for their priorities as they go forth into the world.

THE POWER OF A FATHER'S TALENTS

"And I have filled him with the Spirit of God, in wisdom, in understanding, in knowledge, and in all manner of workmanship."

EXODUS 31:3

As a father, you have been given a powerful influence over those in your family. God, in His divine mercy and infinite wisdom, has also given you certain gifts and talents. How you use them will determine the effect you have on those you love and cherish. A godly father is not easily swayed, but rather is filled with conviction, faith, and prayer. You will gain a sense of your godly responsibility when you choose to stand up for what is right. The Bible encourages you to turn to Him when you need wisdom and strength. Let your intimacy with God guide you in building on the talents you have been given.

YOUR FATHER IS WATCHING;
TAKE ADVANTAGE OF IT

Where can I go from Your Spirit?
Or where can I flee from Your presence?
If I ascend into heaven, You are there;
If I make my bed in hell, behold, You are there.
If I take the wings of the morning,
And dwell in the uttermost parts of the sea,
Even there Your hand shall lead me,
And Your right hand shall hold me.

PSALM 139:7–10

This profound passage in Psalm 139 provides you with all the assurance you need: God has promised that no matter what you are facing or going through, He will be there. When you cannot understand yourself or comprehend your feelings, God invites you to take your internal struggles to Him and ask for His insight. He understands what you do not and knows what to do when you don't. Let each day be filled with the power of His presence, allowing Him to guide you into a deeper relationship with Him. He is your everything.

GODLINESS IN THE FAMILY
BEGINS WITH YOU

Now godliness with contentment is great gain. For we brought nothing into this world, and it is certain we can carry nothing out.

1 TIMOTHY 6:6–7

Contentment is a gift that only God can give. So many times our desire for material possessions overshadows our relationship with God. We can grow content if we see God as our sole provider and focus on the necessities of life. God will often supply our *wants* out of His goodness and grace, but He has promised to supply all of our *needs*. Learn to express your gratitude for what you have and never be concerned about what you are missing. Your greatest source of contentment will be found when you "Delight yourself also in the LORD, And He shall give you the desires of your heart" (Psalm 37:4). Stop for a moment and take inventory of all God has blessed you with and give thanks for each of those blessings.

THE CLEAN RECORD
ONLY GOD CAN GIVE

But if we walk in the light as He is in the light,
we have fellowship with one another, and the blood
of Jesus Christ His Son cleanses us from all sin.

1 JOHN 1:7

The forgiveness of sin is one of God's greatest gifts to those who are in Christ. The slate has been wiped clean, and He has promised to never remember or mention our sins again. Because of God's total, unconditional, overwhelming, and abundant love, He chooses to not only forgive our sins, but also to remove them from His presence forever. The beauty of God's forgiveness opens the door for each of us to have the relationship with Him that He *wants* and we *need*. His love overshadows every sin that we have committed. God's mercy does not give us the freedom to sin, expecting more forgiveness; rather, it gives us the freedom to move past the mistakes we have made and into a deeper, richer relationship with Him and with our loved ones.

A FATHER'S REWARD

*But the fruit of the Spirit is love, joy, peace,
longsuffering, kindness, goodness, faithfulness,
gentleness, self-control. Against such there is no law.*

GALATIANS 5:22–23

As a Christian father, God is calling you to walk in the Spirit in your relationship with those you love and cherish. The transparent life that God wishes you to lead brings out the fruit of the Spirit. Love, joy, peace, patience, kindness, goodness, faithfulness, gentleness, and self-control are all given to you by the Holy Spirit. When the life you lead is God-centered and your relationship with Christ is a priority, the reward you receive is the fruit of the Spirit. Only God can change your heart and give you that certain peace that passes all understanding and reflects the person God wants you to be. Remember, these fruits are not simply one mark of a Spirit-filled life; they are the essence of a Spirit-filled life.

A FATHER'S LEGACY

The righteous man walks in his integrity;
His children are blessed after him.

PROVERBS 20:7

*I*ntegrity—it is such an important word. It helps describe who we are in the Lord and how we are seen by those we love and cherish. It is the foundation of the life we lead and an essential element in our relationship with our heavenly Father. The Lord calls each of us to do what is good and right, to live according to His Word, because godly living reflects His holy character and gives glory to Him. If you choose to become a man of integrity, it will bless your children with a gift that lasts for generations. It would be difficult to think of a greater legacy to leave your loved ones than a personal record of godly integrity.

THE HOME SECURITY SYSTEM

"But whoever listens to me will dwell safely,
And will be secure, without fear of evil."

PROVERBS 1:33

A growing number of people in our world fail to seek God's wisdom. Instead, they strive to satisfy their own selfish passions and desires without a thought for how their actions impact the future or those around them. As a Christian father, this is a spiritually irresponsible and dangerous way to live. If we try to live apart from the counsel of God's wisdom, we will suffer disillusionment, fear, doubt, worry, and frustration. Our lives fall apart when we do not involve the Savior in our decisions. The wisest approach to developing a "home security system" is to seek God daily for His plan, direction, and spiritual insight for our lives.

THE CHARACTER MAKER

And not only that, but we also glory in tribulations,
knowing that tribulation produces perseverance;
and perseverance, character; and character, hope.

ROMANS 5:3–4

A father's character is demonstrated in the way he reacts to hardship, trials, and unpleasant circumstances. God will use trials, difficulties, and adversities to mature you into a person who looks more like His Son. No one enjoys trials, but by faith, you can begin to understand how God may use them as building blocks for strengthening your faith and bringing glory to Him. So, when you think of your life with God, think of the way He wraps you in His loving care. Through your obedience, His loving grace washes over your life like sunlight on a cloudless day when you walk hand-in-hand with God. Though you may face pain and disappointment, nothing can separate you from the presence of God when you choose to walk with Him every day.

THE OPTICAL ILLUSION
ONLY GOD CAN SEE

*While we do not look at the things which are seen, but
at the things which are not seen. For the things which are seen
are temporary, but the things which are not seen are eternal.*

2 CORINTHIANS 4:18

Sometimes we get so caught up in our own day-to-day problems that we lose sight of the big picture that God has planned for our lives. God has given us the task of letting the world know what Jesus has done, which is to make it possible for everyone who has faith in Him to enjoy eternal life and to develop an intimate relationship with the Father. Our day-to-day struggles are only temporary; we must maintain our focus on the eternal. If we truly love the Lord, we will make it our aim and our delight to please Him—by the way we live and by sharing Him with those around us. Look for ways to make Him smile. You have but one life to live for eternity, let it be your best life now.

A FATHER'S PRAYER
CHANGES EVERYTHING

Confess your trespasses to one another, and pray
for one another, that you may be healed. The
effective, fervent prayer of a righteous man avails much.

JAMES 5:16

*S*omeone has said that prayer is like the breath of life: You cannot exist spiritually without it. Prayer is also a great connector in our relationship with other Christian brothers and sisters. God has designed this world in such a way that so many of our needs are met only through mutual interdependence on fellow believers and our singular dependence on God. When a father comes to God in earnest prayer, seeking His will and earnestly bearing his soul for God's direction, his life will be changed and God will be glorified.

THE GOD CONNECTION FOR FATHERS

"If you abide in Me, and My words abide in you, you will ask what you desire, and it shall be done for you. By this My Father is glorified, that you bear much fruit; so you will be My disciples."

JOHN 15:7–8

The only way you can play a significant role in the kingdom of God is to get connected with God and allow Jesus to live His life in and through you—to "abide" in you. The Scripture clearly says in John 15:5 that "without Me you can do nothing." But in Him, you can do anything He calls you to do. You can live out a life of godly example for your children. You can show those around you how to love and glorify the Lord, as well as how to love each other. As His disciple, Jesus calls you to bear much fruit. Through prayer and the study of His Word, seek His guidance daily, and He will reveal that fruit to you.

THE GREAT PHYSICIAN AND YOU

So Jesus answered and said to them, "Assuredly, I say to you,
if you have faith and do not doubt, you will not only do
what was done to the fig tree, but also if you say to this mountain,
'Be removed and be cast into the sea,' it will be done. And
whatever things you ask in prayer, believing, you will receive."

MATTHEW 21:21–22

*S*omeone has said that when you "fight all your battles on your knees, you will win every time." Draw near to God, and you will find healing for your spirit and body when you set aside time to spend with God in prayer. Listen, meditate, and wait upon His direction and guidance. God wants the best for you, and the best is to walk closely with Him in all circumstances, trusting Him in every situation and relationship. This allows your faith to grow and enables you to become the person God wants you to be. James 4:7–8 says, "submit to God. Resist the devil and he will flee from you." God is asking you to take the first step. The Great Physician stands waiting with open arms. Do not hesitate. Run to Him with everything you need today.

PATIENCE AND WISDOM
GO HAND-IN-HAND

He who is slow to anger is better than the mighty,
And he who rules his spirit than he who takes a city.

PROVERBS 16:32

What we say and what we do in our relationships determines who we are with those who are important to us in life. The Bible clearly says in Proverbs 3:13–14, "Happy is the man who finds wisdom, And the man who gains understanding; For her proceeds are better than . . . fine gold." There is a great benefit in learning to be wise and patient with those you have been given the responsibility of nurturing and guiding into adulthood. Children need your wisdom, and they also need to experience your love as you patiently guide them through difficult times. Our culture focuses on "right now," but let godly wisdom and patience guide you as you determine what is best for you and your family.

A FATHER'S LIFESTYLE
IS CONTAGIOUS

But the wisdom that is from above is first pure, then
peaceable, gentle, willing to yield, full of mercy and
good fruits, without partiality and without hypocrisy.

JAMES 3:17

When your lifestyle as a father emulates the love of God and His wisdom, the character you exhibit and the influence you have will impact those who are important to you in life. God's wisdom leads to harmony and peace, while human wisdom leads to arrogance and dissention. Examine yourself: What kind of wisdom do you depend on? Remember, God wants your very best—and so does everyone else you influence, know, and love.

LOOK OUT! SOMEONE IS WATCHING.

The eyes of the LORD are in every place,
Keeping watch on the evil and the good.

PROVERBS 15:3

*T*he thought that someone is watching seldom occurs to us as we go through life. So often, we say what we want and do exactly what we selfishly choose to do. We need to realize that nothing ever escapes the notice of God and nothing ever surprises Him. Proverbs 16:3 says, "Commit your works to the LORD, And your thoughts will be established." When we commit our ways to the Lord, everything changes and pleasing God becomes our priority in life. Because God cares, He wants to bless us with His love and mercy. May your life reflect the love that God so generously gives to those who follow Him.

YOU ARE NOT THE LONE RANGER

Incline your ear and hear the words of the wise,
And apply your heart to my knowledge;
For it is a pleasant thing if you keep them within you;
Let them all be fixed upon your lips,
So that your trust may be in the LORD;
I have instructed you today, even you.

That I may make you know the certainty of the words of truth,
That you may answer words of truth
To those who send to you?

PROVERBS 22:17–19, 21

So many times it is hard to accept that you really *don't* know everything, and the world *does not* rest solely on your shoulders. God openly invites you to listen to the words of His Spirit and open your heart to His knowledge. Take every decision to the Lord, for He stands ready to give the counsel you need. Proverbs 4:10–13 says, "Hear, my son, and receive my sayings, And the years of your life will be many. I have taught you in the way of wisdom; I have led you in right paths. When you walk, your steps will not be hindered, And when you run, you will not stumble. Take firm hold of instruction, do not let go; Keep her, for she is your life." We all need the Lord—you *need* the Lord.

CHANGE IS INEVITABLE; LIVE FOR TODAY

"Do not remember the former things,
Nor consider the things of old.
Behold, I will do a new thing,
Now it shall spring forth;
Shall you not know it?
I will even make a road in the wilderness
And rivers in the desert."

ISAIAH 43:18–19

*B*ad memories belong in your garbage can. You cannot change them, and they will only make you live in the past. God invites you to live for today and for every day in your future. When you have Jesus in your heart, He promises, "if anyone is in Christ, he is a new creation; old things have passed away; behold, all things have become new" (2 Corinthians 5:17). God does not care about your past, your mistakes, or your faults. He also doesn't care about how big your house is, what kind of car you drive, or how full your bank account is; He already owns the world and everything in it. What God does care about—what He really wants from you—is your heart. Give it to Him today!

CULTIVATING CHARACTER IS MORE IMPORTANT THAN CHARISMA

Rather let it be the hidden person of the heart,
with the incorruptible beauty of a gentle and quiet
spirit, which is very precious in the sight of God.

1 PETER 3:4

What would happen in your spiritual life if you spent as much time working on your soul as you do on your golf game, lifting weights, or whatever hobby you are into? Those things *seem* important, but someday they will diminish and die. Your spirit, however, will live forever. Your character is the roadmap of where you have been and where you are going. Let it point the way to the throne of God for it leads your children and those whom you love.

CHOOSE CAREFULLY
THE WORDS YOU SPEAK

Death and life are in the power of the tongue,
And those who love it will eat its fruit.

PROVERBS 18:21

Have you ever considered the impact your words have on your children and those you love? Your words can either build up or destroy their confidence. Your children look to you for love, guidance, and how to cope with growing up in today's world. Choose carefully the words you speak, because the impression you make will greatly impact who your children become. All children need to know they are loved by their earthly father, as well as their heavenly Father. Give the gift of encouragement every day. Psalm 127:3 says, "children are a heritage from the LORD"; be thankful for the blessing of children and share God's love with them today.

STRIVE FOR EXCELLENCE
IN SERVING GOD'S PURPOSE

*And in every work that he began in the service of the
house of God, in the law and in the commandment,
to seek his God, he did it with all his heart. So he prospered.*

2 CHRONICLES 31:21

Excellence in your spiritual life begins with true devotion
to God, which will change you from the inside out. When
the heart changes and pleasing God becomes a priority,
your behavior will also change. And despite what the world
tells you, obedience to the Lord brings more pleasure than
does sin. When you seek the Lord with all of your heart,
you will find him, and the natural result is joyful and earnest obedience to His will. That obedience will bring you
God's blessing and the peace that passes all understanding.

WHAT TO DO WHEN YOU DON'T KNOW WHAT TO DO

He has shown you, O man, what is good;
And what does the LORD require of you
But to do justly,
To love mercy,
And to walk humbly with your God?

MICAH 6:8

Run to the Word when you don't know what to do. Seek His direction for anything and everything. You, as a Christian, are called to be different from the world in the way you live and do business. There should be a clear difference in the way you raise your children. Your marriage should testify to the love of Christ. Those outside the church should be powerfully attracted to the unity and love they see in you and your family. As a believer, you have the responsibility to live in such way that others see Christ in you. As the body of Christ, you are His hands and feet— you are His masterpiece. You may also be the only Jesus some people will ever know.

HUGS AND WORDS OF ENCOURAGEMENT ARE BUILDING BLOCKS FOR THE FAMILY

The heart of the wise teaches his mouth,
And adds learning to his lips.
Pleasant words are like a honeycomb,
Sweetness to the soul and health to the bones.

PROVERBS 16:23–24

*H*ugs and words of encouragement are the building blocks your children need. Their self-image and confidence is dependant on how you interact with them. Make it a habit to hug them often and acknowledge whatever they achieve in school, sports, or the arts. Your presence and open display of affection to your children will help them develop the sense of security they need. Proverbs 23:22 asks your children to "Listen to your father who begot you." Tender, loving words will open the ears of your children, and they will eagerly look to you for wisdom and direction.

A FATHER'S PRIZE IS
REFLECTED IN HIS CHILDREN

Do you not know that those who run in a race all run, but one receives the prize? Run in such a way that you may obtain it.

1 CORINTHIANS 9:24

God has given you a great prize in your children. How you nurture and influence them will shape the man or woman they become. Scripture encourages you to run the race of fatherhood in such a way that you not only receive the prize of salvation for yourself, but that your children do, as well. Proverbs 13:22 says, "A good man leaves an inheritance to his children's children." When your children receive the gift of salvation and experience a personal relationship with Jesus Christ, you have been given the greatest prize a father could receive—to watch your children walk in the Lord. Let your own walk of faith clearly reflect the love of God for all your children to see.

THE GOLDEN RULE FOR FATHERS

"And just as you want men to do to you,
you also do to them likewise."

LUKE 6:31

The world looks at the Golden Rule and declares, "Do unto others before they do it unto you." Our selfish desire to have our own way in life creates a wall between man and God. The Lord encourages you to "love your enemies, do good, and lend, hoping for nothing in return; and your reward will be great" (Luke 6:35). The attitude with which you embrace life will determine the father you become. God knows you from the inside out. Let the chief desire of your heart be to please Him, and by doing so, the way you walk and talk will help others see the love of Christ through you. Living to please God will change everything.

TEACH YOUR CHILDREN
THAT MONEY ISN'T EVERYTHING

How much better to get wisdom than gold!
And to get understanding is to be chosen rather than silver.

PROVERBS 16:16

The love of money touches everyone in life, and we often spend most of our working hours trying to get more. The more we get, the more we want. Our appetite is for material possessions we do not necessarily need. First Timothy 6:9 says, "those who desire to be rich fall into temptation and a snare, and into many foolish and harmful lusts which drown men in destruction and perdition." The Bible condemns the desire to get rich, not because money is a sin, but because money makes a terrible master. People whose primary goal is to get rich serve money—and therefore cannot serve God.

UNCONDITIONAL LOVE
IS THE ONLY OPTION

*So husbands ought to love their own wives as
their own bodies; he who loves his wife loves himself.*

EPHESIANS 5:28

*And you, fathers, do not provoke your children to wrath, but
bring them up in the training and admonition of the Lord.*

EPHESIANS 6:4

*T*he Lord speaks directly to husbands and fathers about
the love and conduct that is so important to both roles.
When you choose to love your wife as you love yourself,
the consideration you give her will deeply affect your
relationship. You, in turn, will receive the respect every
man wants from his wife. Similarly, when you show the
same unconditional love for your children that the Father
extends to you, your children will learn to honor you. The
atmosphere of unconditional love is contagious, and the
security it builds within the home for your wife and your
children will reap great rewards.

A FATHER'S STRESS TEST

Search me, O God, and know my heart;
Try me, and know my anxieties.

PSALM 139:23

There will be times in a father's life when the stress of work, health, family, and friends will test your resolve. Do not make the mistake of thinking you can handle everything by yourself. You are not called to walk through this life alone. The Bible reminds you, "I can do all things through Christ who strengthens me" (Philippians 4:13). Allow Christ to strengthen you. Rest in His Word, "casting all your care upon Him, for He cares for you" (1 Peter 5:7). Seek the Lord, and let the Holy Spirit guide you in every stressful situation.

A TEACHABLE MAN WILL
NEVER STOP GROWING

Go from the presence of a foolish man,
When you do not perceive in him the lips of knowledge.
The wisdom of the prudent is to understand his way,
But the folly of fools is deceit.
Fools mock at sin,
But among the upright there is favor.

PROVERBS 14:7–9

*H*ow long did it take for you to realize you do not know everything? When you come to the realization that there is still much for you to learn, you open the door to becoming a lifelong learner. In your Christian life, God reveals Himself when you surrender to His Word and the leading of His Spirit. Romans 12:2 encourages you to "not be conformed to this world, but be transformed by the renewing of your mind, that you may prove what is that good and acceptable and perfect will of God." God does not simply want you to try harder or sin less, but also to depend on His Spirit and allow yourself to be transformed into someone who loves to please Him through willing obedience. That transformation begins when you choose to become a lifelong learner of God's Word.

A FATHER'S STRENGTH
IS ON HIS KNEES

*"Call to Me, and I will answer you, and show you
great and mighty things, which you do not know."*

JEREMIAH 33:3

Prayer is a very real part of your relationship with God.
It is not just for the special, the religious elite; it is for you.
Throughout the Bible, God promises to speak to you when
you humble yourself and listen for His voice. To listen
actively, you must come before the Lord expectantly. You
must eagerly anticipate Him speaking to you. Get into the
habit of beginning each day with God in prayer; let His
Spirit open your heart and mind to His perfect will. He
promises to "show you great and mighty things, which you
do not know."

A FATHER'S REWARD COMES IN MANY DIFFERENT WAYS

Delight yourself also in the LORD,
And He shall give you the desires of your heart.
Commit your way to the LORD,
Trust also in Him,
And He shall bring it to pass.

PSALM 37:4–5

God wants more than anything else to give you the desires of your heart. You belong to Him, and His love is forever. When you choose to trust Him, He calls you to live in such a way as to honor Him and to do good to others so that they might see God's goodness through you. Your close fellowship with God is the key to a deep commitment to live for Him in every area of your life. He, in turn, wants to bless you. When you delight yourself in the Lord, He places in your heart His desire for you so that you might glorify Him in all that you do.

TRUE PROSPERITY IS THE RECEIPT OF GOD'S REWARD

This Book of the Law shall not depart from your mouth, but you shall meditate in it day and night, that you may observe to do according to all that is written in it. For then you will make your way prosperous, and then you will have good success.

JOSHUA 1:8

When we do God's will, in God's way and with God's help, no one or nothing can stand in the way of our success. The key is the presence of the Lord. God commanded Joshua to meditate on His Word day and night, and He is asking us to do the same today. He wants every father to be prosperous and to be successful in his work and with his family. Yet, He wants you to remember that your true treasures will accumulate in heaven. God's Word is your guide to life. When you discover His wisdom and apply it to your life, everything changes. Your focus, priorities, emotions, and heart become God-centered. When this occurs, you and your family will be so very blessed, and in whatever you choose to do, you will receive God's richest rewards of peace, guidance, salvation, and an eternity spent with Him.

GOD LISTENS TO A FATHER'S PRAYER WHEN …

YOU ASK FOR PATIENCE: Colossians 3:21; James 1:2–4; Hebrews 12:1; Philippians 2:1–4

YOU ASK FOR HIS SPIRIT'S GUIDANCE: Romans 8:31–32; Psalm 143:10–11; 2 Corinthians 3:17–18; Psalm 91:11–16

YOU ADMIT YOUR SHORTCOMINGS AS A FATHER: Psalm 71:12, 15–18; Deuteronomy 28:1–4; Jeremiah 33:3; Proverbs 15:29–33

YOU ARE OVERWHELMED BY YOUR RESPONSIBILITIES: Psalm 127:1–5; Isaiah 40:26; Isaiah 43:2, 5–7; Deuteronomy 31:6; Isaiah 54:10

NO ONE ELSE WILL LISTEN: Matthew 7:7–8; 1 Thessalonians 5:16–18; 2 Chronicles 7:14; Psalm 4:1

YOU CONFESS YOUR SIN AND SEEK FORGIVENESS: Proverbs 15:29–33; Hebrews 8:12; Ephesians 1:6–7; Proverbs 28:13

YOU PUT THE LORD FIRST IN YOUR LIFE: 1 Peter 5:6–7; Proverbs 2:1–5; Psalm 18:1–3; James 4:7–8

YOU BRING YOUR PROBLEMS TO HIM: 1 Peter 3:12–15; Matthew 19:26; 2 Corinthians 1:9–10; 2:14–17

WORRY AND DOUBT THREATEN YOUR WELL-BEING: Psalm 145:15–21; Isaiah 26:3; Psalm 128:1–6; Psalm 68:19

YOU TRUST AND WAIT FOR GOD'S ANSWERS: Psalm 62:5–8; Isaiah 45:5–6; James 1:16–17; Proverbs 30:5; Zephaniah 3:1

GOD'S PROMISES FOR FATHERS

ETERNAL LIFE: John 3:14–17; 1 John 2:24–25; Hebrews 2:9–15; 1 Corinthians 15:51–57

SAFETY: Psalm 33:12–20; Psalm 9:9–12; 1 Peter 5:7–11; Psalm 121:1–8

PEACE: Isaiah 26:2–4; John 14:27; John 16:33; Psalm 119:162–165; Romans 5:1–2

COMFORT: Psalm 94:17–19; Psalm 119:50–52; Isaiah 40:1–2, 4–5; 2 Corinthians 1:3–7

POWER: Philippians 4:1, 11–13; Isaiah 40:28–31; John 14:11–13; Ephesians 3:13–16, 20–21

JUSTICE: Psalm 37:1–3; Psalm 7:6–11, 17; Psalm 26:1–3, 6; 1 Corinthians 4:2–5

WISDOM: James 1:5–6; Proverbs 2:1–7; Proverbs 3:13–18; 1 Corinthians 1:26–31

FORGIVENESS: Romans 8:1–2; 1 John 1:9; Colossians 1:12–14; Psalm 103:10–12

GOD'S BLESSINGS
FOR FATHERS WITH ...

LOVE: Ephesians 3:17–19; Isaiah 43:1–4; Zephaniah 3:17; Titus 3:4–8

STRENGTH: Psalm 28:7–9; Psalm 29:1–4, 9–11; Psalm 46:1–5; Isaiah 41:10; 2 Corinthians 12:9–10

JOY: Habakkuk 3:17–19; Psalm 5:11–12; Luke 2:10–14; Isaiah 51:3, 11

FRUITFULNESS: John 15:1–9; Galatians 5:22–26; Colossians 1:9–10; Proverbs 8:19–21

HIS SPIRIT: Romans 8:9–10; Psalm 33:18–22; 1 Corinthians 2:10–16; 2 Corinthians 3:5–6

HOPE: Romans 15:13; Psalm 33:18–22; John 16:33; Ephesians 4:2–6; Lamentations 3:22–24

GUIDANCE: Isaiah 48:17; Isaiah 58:11; Psalm 32:8; John 16:13; Ezekiel 36:27

RESPONSIBILITIES
OF FATHERHOOD TO …

BE A MAN OF INTEGRITY: Psalm 1:1–6; Psalm 112:5–7; Psalm 119:1–8; Proverbs 11:1–3; Proverbs 12:17–19

INSTRUCT YOUR CHILDREN IN HIS WORD: Proverbs 4:1–4; Psalm 78:1–8; Proverbs 1:5–9; Proverbs 8:32–35

TEACH YOUR CHILDREN TO PRAY: Matthew 6:5–13; 1 John 5:13–15; Romans 8:24–28; Isaiah 65:24

TEACH YOUR CHILDREN GRATITUDE: Deuteronomy 31:13; Deuteronomy 3:19–21; Philippians 4:8–11; Psalm 30:4–6

SHOW KINDNESS TO YOUR FAMILY: Matthew 7:9–11; Joshua 2:12–14; Ephesians 4:31–32; 1 Thessalonians 2:10–12

SPEAK ENCOURAGING WORDS: Ephesians 4:29–32; James 3:2–10; Matthew 12:34b, 36–37; Romans 14:7–19

TRUST GOD WHEN YOU DON'T UNDERSTAND: Psalm 121:4–8; Romans 11:33–36; Psalm 86:7–10; Proverbs 30:5

GOD'S DYNAMIC
EXAMPLE OF FATHERS

ABRAHAM: Genesis 12:1–3; Genesis 13:14–16; Genesis 15:1–6; Genesis 17:1–5; Genesis 21:1–8

JACOB: Psalm 78:65–72; Genesis 32:24–30; Genesis 35:1–3; Genesis 37:32–35

JOSEPH—JACOB'S SON: Genesis 41:50–57; Genesis 45:1–10; Genesis 47:12; Genesis 48:8–10

DAVID: Psalm 132:8–18; 2 Samuel 22:1, 29–36; 1 Chronicles 28:20; 2 Chronicles 7:17–18

MANOAH—SAMSON'S FATHER: Judges 13:1–7, 24–25

ZACHARIAS—JOHN'S FATHER: Luke 1:5–15, 57-64, 67–68, 80

NOAH: Genesis 5:29; Genesis 6:7–10; Genesis 7:23–8:1; Genesis 9:1, 8–9

JOSEPH—MARY'S HUSBAND: Matthew 1:18–25; Matthew 2:13-14, 19–21

CRISIS SCRIPTURE GUIDE

ADDICTION: Galatians 5:1; John 8:32; Proverbs 20:1

AGING: Proverbs 9:11; Ecclesiastes 11:10; Proverbs 10:27

ANGER: 1 Peter 2:23; Ephesians 4:26–27; 1 Thessalonians 5:9

ANXIETY: John 14:27; Philippians 4:6–8; Psalm 46:1–3

BACKSLIDING: Proverbs 28:13; Psalm 51:10–12; John 6:37

BEREAVEMENT: 1 Corinthians 15:54–57; Isaiah 25:8; 1 Thessalonians 4:13–14

BITTERNESS: Ephesians 4:31; Hebrews 12:15; James 3:14–15

CARNALITY: Romans 6:6–9; Ephesians 4:22–24; 2 Corinthians 4:16

CONDEMNATION: Romans 8:1; Romans 3:10–12; Isaiah 64:6–8

CONFUSION: Isaiah 26:3; 1 Corinthians 14:33; Isaiah 55:8–9

DEATH: Romans 14:7–8; Job 19:25-27; Isaiah 25:8

DEPRESSION: Nehemiah 8:10; Philippians 4:8; Romans 8:28

DISSATISFACTION: Proverbs 27:20; Hebrews 13:5–6; 1 Timothy 6:6–8

DOUBT: James 4:8; Romans 10:17; Hebrews 10:32, 35–39

FAILURE: Proverbs 24:16–18; Psalm 145:14–16; 2 Corinthians 3:5

FEAR: 2 Timothy 1:7; Philippians 4:13; Revelation 1:17–18

FINANCES: Matthew 6:31–34; Psalm 37:25–26; Philippians 4:19

ILLNESS: James 5:14; Psalm 23:2–4; Psalm 43:5

INSECURITY: 2 Thessalonians 3:3; Psalm 91:3–7; 2 Corinthians 3:4–5

JUDGING: 1 Corinthians 4:5; Matthew 7:3–5; John 5:22

LONELINESS: John 14:18; Psalm 147:3; Psalm 27:10

LUST: 2 Peter 2:9; Matthew 18:8–9; Proverbs 6:25–26

MARRIAGE: 2 Corinthians 6:14–17; 1 Corinthians 7:10–17; Hebrews 13:4

PRIDE: Matthew 18:2–4; Proverbs 27:1–2; Luke 18:11–14

SATAN: Ephesians 6:10–17; 1 John 4:1–3; Luke 10:18–19

SUFFERING: Hebrews 5:8–9; 2 Corinthians 4:8–10; 1 Peter 4:19

TEMPTATION: James 1:12; 1 Peter 4:12–13; Psalm 34:17

WEAKNESS: 2 Corinthians 12:9; Matthew 11:28–30; Psalm 121:2–3

WORLDLINESS: Mark 4:18–20; 1 John 5:5; 1 John 2:15–17

NOTES

NOTES

NOTES

NOTES

NOTES